Five Degrees To

Your Future

Shift Your Course, Transform Your Life,

Do More Of What You Love!

Dr. Cathy Hunter, D.C.

ISBN: 979-8-9899788-0-9

DEDICATION

This book would not be possible without the love and support of my husband Larry, as well as my dear friends and family. The list is so long...but to name a few: Amber, Angie, Jeni, Jennifer, Krissy K, Karen, Karin, Kim, Lynn, Peter, Sue, and Toni. I do not want to leave anyone out, so if you do not see your name, you know who you are and I am forever grateful for you. A huge thank you to my niece, Brittany Hunter for helping edit this book and her unwavering support, as well as my dear friend, Angela Herrera, for her heartfelt forward.

For My Mom & Dad
for giving me life and all the ups and downs that came with it to support and challenge me to grow into what I am today.

CONTENTS

FOREWORD

Why are we drawn to certain people? Do you have that one person or perhaps several people in your life that have changed it so drastically you could not imagine your life without them? Dr. Cathy Hunter, Hunter, or sometimes Hunts as I call her, has been that influence in mine.

When I first met Hunter, she was my boss. She owned a Chiropractic clinic and I was hired as an assistant. I was barely twenty-one at the time. My first impression of her was that she was a bit crazy, but definitely that good unexplainable crazy! I remember thinking she was different and so refreshing. Hunter intrigued me with her infectious personality, and I speedily noticed everyone she interacted with loved her. I loved my new job and relished in learning from Hunter.

The relationship I formed with my employer developed into joining the soccer team she was on, crafting together at her house, and ultimately led to her inspiring me to run. I remember initially thinking it was quite odd she would go for a run on her lunch break and then return to the office as if it was something people "normally" did. Observing Hunter do all these extraordinary things inspired me to take part. Before meeting Hunter, I never enjoyed running outside of a soccer game, in fact it was a task I once thought of as agonizing. Hunter, being a natural encourager, gave me the knowledge I needed to become a runner.

My connection to her grew and so did my love for running. Hunter inspired me to challenge myself as I never had before. Running my first 10k race turned into us training together for a full marathon, yes, 26.2 miles! Hunter had always been an experienced runner. With hard work and dedication, I began to develop my skill as well. Everything I watched her do I wanted to do as well, I suddenly felt limitless. For the first time in my life, I felt in total control of my mind and body.

Our short runs turned to long runs and our chats at work became deep conversations, sometimes hours at length. We have celebrated together and grieved together. Hunter's unique perspective on life has guided me through many of my own challenges.

Looking back at my life the past twenty years it was the small shifts that led to each success. The "shifts" are exactly what Hunter describes in this book. Taking a chance at a new job, led to an amazing friendship. Beginning to run, led to full marathon. Lifestyle is a choice; you can obtain anything when small shifts are made – five degrees turns into ten degrees and before you realize it a large shift in your life has been made and becomes routine.

If I think of the Cathy Hunter I met almost twenty years ago I would have never thought she had any room for improvement, she seemed perfect in every way. To watch her grow and direct her life in the path she had always imagined has been a pleasure to watch and take part in. Hunter made changes even when she experienced fear and uncertainty, and the outcome was truly magical for her. She literally created her own private oasis when she needed a moment to pause and process.

Hunter has overcome business challenges, a difficult divorce, and dealt with the death of loved ones – all while navigating the never-ending mental struggles that always seem to tag along! Through all of life's expected and unexpected challenges she has been able to rise above and come out stronger.

Hunter is not only my dear friend but my mentor. Everyone around her is drawn to her and her love for life and healing others radiates! It's like you can never get enough of her!

We have literally ran together for thousands of miles, some miles full of laughter while others full of tears. As a Chiropractor, Hunter not only treats her patients physically but she has built friendships and deep connections with many. Hunter's passion for others shows in all she does and she is continuously seeking more ways to help and heal.

I am certain you will love this book as much as I loved watching the process in real time. Through reading her story and making small shifts as she explains in this book you too can rise above any challenge, after all, being the best version of ourselves is truly the Hunter way!

– Angela Herrera

Mother, Wife, Runner & Living My Best Life

1 PREFACE

This book is at least twenty years in the making. Yes, you read that correctly: Twenty years! It has not been an idle two decades, however. I have pondered, written notes and chapters, gathered information, and most importantly of all, dreamt of the finished copy. I've lost track of how many books I've read, courses I invested in, and webinars I attended, all for the purpose of getting me on track to finally becoming an author. And for twenty years, I have admittedly chickened out. Until now...

Leading up to writing this book, there were lots of different books. Some looked similar to what I am writing now, some were on totally different subjects (hello shiny object syndrome). In these seemingly random manuscripts, I hacked away at various subjects; holistics, the power of positivity, manifestation, etc. At the time, I thought they were useless endeavors of writing chaos and endless tangents. They left me frustrated and bereft, each one feeling farther from my goal than the last. All of the harsh self-critics out there can relate to this cycle. All my doubt and rumination overshadowed the true feat of these attempts: they were all really small steps to actually doing it. It was this revelation that got me thinking about the impact of small shifts and changes in our lives.

Most significant changes in our lives happen like that, in small steps. Of course there are big events that can alter the direction we are headed: death, divorce, getting fired, etc. Most outcomes occur by taking small, incremental modifications that eventually gain momentum and get us the very things we have hoped and dreamed for. Often, these changes masquerade as perceived inopportunity.

2020 was a year that we will all remember as one of the craziest, uncertain, unprecedented years we have ever experienced. Of course in of the wackiest years, 2020, I hit the big milestone of turning 50. My friends and I had planned a Puerto Vallarta getaway. It was signed, sealed, and all but delivered before the advent of the pandemic. We collectively decided to cancel because we wanted to be safe and traveling to another county seemed too sketchy at the time. I also did not think it was prudent to end up taking off almost three weeks of work given the time we were gone and the additional fourteen days we were supposed to quarantine when we returned home. It was during this time something shifted in my brain as I crossed this half a century threshold. I didn't care anymore. Not in an apathetic way, but more so in what others thought about my writing and ideas. It wasn't until I finally cast aside my fears and reservations did I feel liberated enough to write what you're reading now. *What an epiphany*, I thought. Only it wasn't. Upon further inspection, I realized it was not all of the sudden, but years of small changes and shifts that finally led me here.

I grew up in the smallish town of Sayreville, New Jersey. It is something that I am very proud of, and as they say "you can take the girl out of Jersey, but you can't take the Jersey out of the girl". As a kid I wanted to be everything from; some kind of doctor, either an MD, or veterinarian, a genetic engineer, astronaut, or first base-woman for the New York Yankees (still waiting on my call up to the majors). In the end, I found my path after injuring myself as a varsity runner in high school. It was a chiropractor that alleviated my pain and allowed me to continue my running. As a result, I not only became a chiropractor, but I am still an avid runner.

Knowing that I wanted to be a chiropractor when I was in high school directed my schooling path. First I went off to Rutgers College in New Brunswick, NJ. I graduated in 1992 and took the next year to knock off a few more prerequisite classes at Middlesex County

College (oh the dreaded Organic Chemistry I and II). During this year I also was a server at a local seafood restaurant where I worked my butt off and saved as much money as I could.

With a few suitcases and some money saved, in 1993, I began chiropractic school in Whittier, California at Los Angeles College of Chiropractic. Although I immersed myself in school and followed around my mentor doctor, Dr. Richard Gohl, DC, I realized toward the end of my first year this school was not for me. I absolutely loved California, but after a trip to Iowa to see "The Fountainhead", which is Palmer College of Chiropractic, I knew I had to transfer. I moved to Iowa, had to repeat many classes that I already took and got

7

A's in ("these classes are different at Palmer", blah blah), but did it anyway and finally graduated in 1997. I found a way to finish my clinical requirements in two versus three trimesters so I could once again return to California and intern with my mentor doctor, Dr. Gohl, in Glendale, CA for my final trimester.

I did not realize how difficult practicing would be. Chiropractic is an art, science, and a philosophy. At 26, I was running my own practice with absolutely no idea how to put it all together. I struggled financially, mentally (I could have chosen any career and I chose one that I felt that I could not succeed at!) and physically made myself sick as I tried to figure it all out.

My lack of success and frustration led me to

"practice jump" all the time. I would have my own practice (which entailed renting rooms in other doctor's offices at 50% of my income), and was responsible for figuring out my own marketing to bring in patients to see me and then actually knowing what to do with them. Being so young with very little experience was such a mind f**k. I was a trained doctor, worked hard on my chiropractic adjusting and therapies, but my lack of confidence prevented me from solidifying myself as an authority on their health or just about anything. I moved my location all over the map – in California: Glendale, Venice Beach, Solana Beach, Del Mar; then I did a stint in Aruba (best time of my life!); then back to Del Mar. Eventually, I landed a job in San Francisco.

The job entailed running a multi-million dollar clinic in downtown San Francisco. Needless to say the money and opportunity were things I could not turn down. So, I left Southern California for the Bay Area. It was the hardest I ever worked up to that point, but what I learned allowed me to eventually move to Simi Valley where I have lived and thrived ever since. Our practice in Simi Valley even had different locations over time. Three with my business partner at the time, and two when I went back to solo practice. This last location has brought me to my home office, a dream my husband has made come true for me.

The summer before I left for chiropractic school, I remember having dinner with friends on a beautiful summer night by the ocean. As we sipped our cocktails, we all told each other our dreams of what we wanted for our lives. I told my friends that when I became a chiropractor, I wanted to be that "home town doctor", a modern day Marcus Welby. I would live where I practiced, hopefully having my office on my property and taking care of families; parents, grandparents, children, where I was known and loved. This dream has finally come true here in Simi Valley. I had no idea it would take 27 years and tons of small alterations in my life that would all accumulate to the place I stand today. I could not, and did not, get to my dream career right away or with giant changes in my life. It is the small steps that kept me moving forward, sometimes jutting left, sometimes veering right. All of the little steps added up over time, and forged a wonderful adventure and a proud place to land. If I kept thinking of how daunting it would be to get to my ultimate goal, I would have just given up. Instead, I kept plugging along, making small changes and building my way to the top.

It is funny how time rolls on, and you start to notice things that took a while to settle in. In particular, the last couple of years I realized when I am interacting with my patients, they are actually listening. That may sound silly given a majority of these dear people have been with me the 18 years I have been practicing in Simi Valley. I guess it took this long for me to really notice that we are doing more than adjusting their spines and helping to improve their health. We are going deeper; talking about life's trials and tribulations, sharing intimate events that add to our existence, advice and camaraderie. I am free flowing ideas with them, based on my experience both professionally and personally, and they are listening. My openness about my life and genuine advice and storytelling helps and inspires my patients with their own goals and changes they want to obtain. They even help me with what they share in our time together.

At 26 years old, it seemed like no one cared what I had to say about health, let alone life. None of my patients wanted to hear it from a kid with very little chiropractic and life experiences. That was part of the bigger reason I struggled for six years getting my practice and my life together. One thing I learned through all of my career is that I love helping people. There is something about getting people to smile, even with strangers, that warms my heart. It has truly been a blessing to help people with their health and lives and sharing my life with them in hopes they can be inspired and improve themselves.

My path has finally come to this point: to move beyond the four walls of my office and venture out into the world to help as many people as I can. I have had many mentors and teachers along the way that have prepared me to extend my touch to the world. Most recently, I would like to thank Sam Crowley of Everydayissaturday.com. He has motivated me to grab life by the horns on a daily basis and finally make this dream of writing and podcasting a reality. Sam has also taught me invaluable insights and stream line technical aspects of podcasting and I am so excited for my podcasting future. I would also like to give a shout out to Chandler Bolt of Self-publishingschool.com for writing epic books like "Published". I have finally followed his plan to write my own book. His books, webinars and interactions have been vital to my success. I want to inspire people to go for whatever they want in their life. However big, like a career, or however small, like stop eating so much junk food, but whatever they really want. I've had so much help over the years from family, friends, mentors and strangers and now it is my time to broaden my reach.

We all know where our parade is headed: to our final resting place on this earth. Life flies by, whether you are having fun or not. So why not go for what you want, enjoy your journey, and live your best life. Your goals are just a step – by step, by step, by step – away. You have to start and not get overwhelmed. If I can write this book, you can do anything. And I am here to inspire you to do that in your own life.

2 FOUNDATION

So what is it you want to do? Is there anything you want to accomplish? I am asking YOU. Not what others want you to do, or what you should do, or what is expected of you. None of these. What is it that you *really* want?

Sometimes in life we play roles; act the way we should, or how we are expected to be in life. We sacrifice our time, energy and want people around us to be OK. There is a time and place for all of that, but now it is *your* time.

Whatever you want to accomplish can be big or small. Any burning desires? Any dreams you have not fulfilled yet? It could be something seemingly small, like to start walking more. So here is the next question: why haven't you done it yet? Have you even started taking steps toward it?

This book is only the beginning. It is a road map to accomplish anything you want to have, be, or do in your life. The best part about this book, and the road map I am sharing with you, is that it can be applied over and over again to any goal you want to achieve. When you examine this outline, you can use it to live your best life, you can look back at all that you have already accomplished and realize you have been doing this type of thing repeatedly during your life.

When you start on a path to achieving anything, it is easy to get overwhelmed. Whether it is a life altering habit you want to form, or limiting watching television night after night. Sometimes it is hard to see the proverbial forest through the trees. Having this book as your guide, all you have to do is go back to small steps versus focusing on the "how the heck am I going to really make this happen!" Take it one day, one chunk, one win at a time. Watch your progress grow, slowly at first, but then gain incredible momentum. You will be looking back with a big 'ole grin and wonder why you hadn't done that sooner!

Being the woman who wears not only rose colored sunglasses, but ones adorned with sparkles, I live by the motto: anything is possible. That being said, you still have to set a course and take action towards your destination. This is nothing new, but small changes will eventually produce big outcomes. As these results come into your being, they naturally become part of your normal life.

Remember when you were learning to tie your shoes? Ride a bike? Learn your ABCs? Now all of those mundane things just flow normally and you cannot imagine not being able to do them. I am no exception in my own life. Altering my course, little increments over time, have got me here: in my career, being an avid runner, and keeping my excellent health. Over the pages of this book, I will share examples in my own life's journey to show you it can be done, and to inspire you to materialize your own desires.

This is exactly how I wrote this book: I made a plan, I wrote daily. Pages became chapters, chapters became the entire book, the rough draft got edited and well, you are reading it right now. Every day writing became easier, flowed more naturally and dare I say, became enjoyable and something to look forward to. I was so scared of writing, procrastinated for years until I followed my own advice and now I am so glad I did!

As you shift your course in life, the new slightly altered direction will spark new shifts. Changes that you may not even previously thought about, or ones that you did not realize you wanted to bring about. Another magical thing that happens on your newly altered path are the revelations that emerge. Feelings, attitudes, opinions, both directly and indirectly are brought to light. A lot of the time, it is like a light bulb going on and you cannot believe you did not think of it this way before. Views on the world get broader and brighter. You may even get some closure on past issues or figure out new ways to deal with old beliefs. Yes, life gets its spark back. The magic is revealed. And you have yourself to thank for all of it.

Well, are you excited? I am! So let's get to it...

3 SMALL CHANGES HUGE EFFECTS

When you are making a change in your life, whatever that change may be, if it is too big of a change, it can quickly become daunting. As this massive alteration in your life is looming, the sheer amount of energy you have to put forth to create this change may be too hard to stick with because of its size alone.

When one becomes overwhelmed, it is easy to simply give up. What is worse, you keep plugging along, giving it "half-ass" effort. Whether the task at hand is too overwhelming, or you mind numbingly surrender to

your path that ultimately goes nowhere. Either way, you do not get the desired outcome you set out for. So, we need to piecemeal the process so it becomes palatable and we get the job done.

Five Degrees, Not 180 degrees

If you want to consistently conquer any goal, you need to make small shifts that ultimately get you to the finish line. You want to cross this milestone with a proud, strong demeanor, versus being so exhausted you do not get to savor your accomplishment. By making small shifts, heading five degrees in your existing course, you can carry out the necessary changes, piece by piece to arrive at your destination. It is a hell of a lot easier to train weekly for a marathon rather than jumping in the morning of the race and prodding painfully through the entire 26.2 miles.

Five Degrees – Mentally Easier

Our minds are in control of our bodies, mental health, and destinies. The mind is constantly figuring out ways to survive and thrive in our world. Our minds also love to win. It enjoys a winning process, not a struggle filled with failures and heartache. Although obstacles and failure are imminent as you try to hit your goals, it is so important to set yourself up for success as much as you can.

Shifting five degrees, you can give your mind a break and allow its powerful self to make changes, make them stick, and accomplish what you want. With this game plan, you can "trick" your mind into accepting this is just how it is, how you are, what you do, etc. Have you ever tried to eat better, maybe something as simple as using quinoa rather than rice for your meals? Besides the fact it tastes good (my biased opinion), soon after you use this swap, it becomes very natural to have quinoa as your go to grain. Your mind goes, "ah, OK, this is what we cook now". I am not saying you never have rice again, or you do not dream of non-quinoa dishes, but it develops into a normal routine for you. The mind is adaptable, and it appreciates smaller changes that it can actually execute and accept. What we are doing here is laying down the tracks to form a habit. Google defines habit as, "a settled or regular tendency or practice, especially one that is hard to give up." That is what we are going for: a change that becomes part of your life and one you want to do. We have all heard debate about how long it really takes to form a habit that is long term. Is it 20 days? 60? 90? In my opinion there is no hard rule. Mr. Google says 18 to 254 days. Mr. Google also points out that it takes an average of 66 days to become automatic. Talk about five degrees to somewhere! The point is, it takes time.

That time depends on the person, their mindset and

how badly they want what they are after. So it makes

perfect sense to shift your course slightly...swap out

the quinoa for other grains in your meals...and before

you know it, you will be a quinoa master!

Five Degrees – Physically Easier

If your goal is something in the physical realm, say

regular running or lifting weights, you have to get your

body used to it. Muscles need time to learn new

movements (or revisit old ones), and recover properly.

I know if I have not run in a week or so, my first couple

DR. CATHY HUNTER, D.C.

of easy runs make me so sore and a bit discouraged. So I try to spread them out, and have off days where I just walk and stretch so I get back in the swing of things.

By starting off on a smaller scale, you also lessen your chance of injury. Nothing is worse than hurting yourself when you are starting on a regular exercise regimen. Not only is it painful, but it hinders you because you need to back off while you heal and that in of itself takes time.

Recently, we started playing more golf. A usually easy par three, nine-hole course turns into being sore and icing for several days. I should have gone to the driving range a few days a week for a few weeks then hit the 9 hole links. Physically, you need to build up endurance as well. I have been discouraged in the past from lifting weights (small ones!) because I get so sore. Not only am I in pain, but it makes it difficult to deliver effective chiropractic care because I have to be fast to adjust someone's spine. The painful, sore muscles slow my reaction time down. So, I instilled a weight lifting program using light weights, more repetitions and sets, two to three times a week. This program allowed me to handle the resultant soreness and not affect my quality of chiropractic care.

Five Degrees – Emotionally Easier

Emotions are the feelings that you experience versus

what we refer to as mentally, which is how your mind processes and understands things. Negative emotions can stop us dead in our tracks. One of the worst feelings when you are trying to get things done is being overwhelmed. This can make you throw your hands in the air and give the whole thing up.

When you chunk a task down to smaller parts, you start to gain momentum. This gives you a euphoric feeling and fills you with hope and strength to keep going. It also keeps the overburden at bay by preventing it because you are crossing things off your list. This also prevents boredom. If your goal is too large and you do not break it down into realistic pieces, it loses its luster and makes you yawn. Being bored is a terrible feeling too and it is definitely not productive.

I often self-diagnose myself with shiny object syndrome. I will be working on one project when another idea will spark in my head and it looks so shiny and new...before you know it, I drop what I was working on and start following this new idea. Although it is fun to be filled with so many ideas and creative energy, it is actually a detriment to accomplishing the goals I wanted in the first place. I am learning to keep a running list of things I want to achieve, but take the time to get to the current end goal or make the regular changes so it becomes a habit before diving into something new. Like writing this book.

It is emotionally stimulating to witness small progressions and realize, "hey, I am really getting it done!". Admiring our own development gives us a happiness boost filled with energy to keep going. It gets me excited to look back at all the chapters I have written and smile that words are flowing and I really will finish this book. Building excitement in the journey to your goal is the fuel to keep it fun and push you towards finishing it.

Christopher Columbus – he pulled an accidental five degrees. The main purpose of his epic journey was to search for a direct ocean route to travel from Europe to Asia. As the history books tell us, he never accomplished that mission. He did not leave Europe and turn west, or 180 degrees, but he made small course changes and impacted history. Instead of a more direct water trade route, he discovered the Americas. As we know, there were already people inhabiting these lands, but this area was primarily undiscovered for most Europeans.

Historians believe he initially landed on an island in the Bahamas. Columbus' change of course (small errors actually) ended up sparking a vast exploration of the Americas. Sadly, his journey ushered in a lot of exploitation as well. However, what if Columbus never landed in the Americas and instead found his water route? We can only speculate what the world would be like today. It makes you think: what five degrees can you alter in your own course to bring about a host of possibilities?

Consistency and Cumulative Effects

Once you shift your own five degrees, you need to do a little bit everyday. Each day keeps adding up, and that builds powerful momentum. Your small shift begins to gain traction and before you know it, you have some big time changes happening. Days stack onto each other, and cumulative effects begin to take hold. It is a magical process to watch. Something you really wanted to accomplish that may have seemed unattainable begins to take shape. As you gain ground in your endeavor, it makes it easier to continue down this five degree path.

Another interesting cumulative effect is as you continue down your path, and you have a lot of repetitive behaviors under your belt, this tends to awaken other shifts and revelations. You may not have even thought of them before, or this new trajectory is opening your eyes to other possibilities. Either way, the energy that you are expounding to accomplish your goal is becoming automatic and this leaves more mind power to explore other ideas. Who knows what you will come up with as you set out on your course!

4 RUNNING

I was basketball obsessed in elementary school and into my tweens. I played constantly. My coveted basketball was with me at all times, I loved to clean it, hold it, and embrace how it felt. It was a smaller ball at first because I was so small. It made me so happy especially because I convinced my mother to actually buy me one. We had a basketball hoop at my grandmother's house. It was so much fun to be outside and play "horse" with my cousins and brother whenever I could. I dreamt of being a professional basketball player, even though there were no major professional women's leagues at the time. Playing with the men seemed perfectly feasible to me.

As a perpetually small child, I was born five pounds, five ounces (five is a recurring number in my life). I did not let this stop me in sports as a kid: I played softball in a recreation league and a basketball elementary league. When I began junior high, (yes, I am dating myself, I know now we call it middle school) I played seventh and eighth grade junior high basketball which was in the winter season. I also ran middle school spring track, but I remember it being more of an introduction to a track team versus a true competitive schedule of meets. In track, I believe the farthest I ever competitively ran was the 880 yard or half mile, nowadays it is referred to as the 800 meter. I enjoyed running farther distances over shorter sprints. Due to my boundless energy, I worked hard in all my sports.

Junior High was seventh through ninth grade back then and the school was just up the hill from our high school. In ninth grade we could continue to play junior high basketball or try out for JV, junior varsity, basketball and play with the JV high school team. I wanted to accelerate my game and I knew I had to give it a shot and see if I could make the team. Talking to upperclassmen, the norm was to run XC, cross country, in the fall. It was the vehicle for kids to get in shape for basketball, even if you were a terrible runner. It seemed like they let anyone join the team, the more grueling runners the better.

My plan was to run XC merely to be in the best shape for JV basketball, and hopefully make the team. So, I signed up for XC and could not imagine what would happen next, given my limited experience with running versus my longer history with basketball. So, this five degree shift in my life had me running with the elite seniors the first week. I loved it! Who would have known that I happened to be a naturally talented long distance runner?!

I became a Varsity freshman which was a difficult, high pressure thing to do. Our XC coach, Mrs. Carney, along with her husband Mr. Carney (who coached XC and basketball in our neighboring town) took me under their collective wings. He would run solo with me through our towns and teach me pace and form. Sometimes it was painful and annoying, but he sure did know what he was doing.

They took me to XC Junior Olympic races all over the state. I placed in the top ten percent over and over again, sometimes in fields of hundreds of other girls. It was a special time in my young life. To be around mentors and coaches who loved me for my running skills, as well as a silly kid really meant a lot to me. It was fantastic! It was bigger than just running. It gave me confidence and was way more fun than my broken home life.

My father passed away when I was nine years old. Following my father's departure, my older brother fell into drugs, drinking, and trouble right after that. This left my mother devoting all her time to chasing after him and me to my own devices. I realize now my coaches really saved my butt and gave me a direction that could have been sadly different without their love and support. In fact, my mom only came to about 4 of my meets in my whole four year running career.

That first magical XC season was filled with winning, accolades and accomplishments. Right after that, I ironically made the JV basketball team. Even with my XC super training, I remember being so sore during the tryouts, using different muscles and feeling every fiber. They made me the ball handler, which was a point guard that helped direct the game. It was fun and I was good at it. I even had moments of being very good, but I was not great. I got a taste of greatness in XC and I longed for more. I was still small and skinny, and I believe all the cardiovascular training from XC running just pushed that issue.

Being a small giraffe did not help my confidence or my ability in basketball. As a result, I was losing my passion for basketball that had been with me for years. That fire was replaced with long distance running and the talent I had for it. That first XC season led to varsity XC all four years, as well as four years of varsity long distance spring track and three varsity long distance winter track seasons. I mainly ran the mile and two mile for the track seasons which was very difficult because I had to perform in both races each meet. XC was three mile races and I excelled better with the longer distance, either winning or ranking close to the top.

My junior year in high school I got hurt from running. All of the sudden my knees and hips were painful and burning, even when I was not actually running. My coaches panicked that their star runner was in trouble and immediately brought me to a medical doctor to see what was going on. This doctor examined me and took x-rays. Thank goodness it was negative for fracture or pathology. This left the doctor confused as to why I was injured. So, he told my coaches maybe my injury was in my mind, because possibly I could not handle the mental pressure of being number one on my teams. The doctor's conclusion was the farthest from the truth. It was a major blow to my confidence and emotional health. Especially when the coaches were siding more with that than a physical reason I was hurt.

I was in pain; could not run without pain, pain without running. I could not perform as I used to. It was devastating and it appeared the very people who cared so much for me were now looking for their next running star. My mother told me just to quit XC and track all together. That seemed to be her mantra when things got tough. My whole positive world was running and it was crumbling right before my eyes.

During this time, my brother got in a bad car accident. He was seeing a chiropractor for the injuries he sustained. Even though we had a strained relationship because of his troubled choices, I still looked up to him. He recommended I go see his doctor. I did not understand how this chiropractor could help me when the MD I had seen could not find anything wrong with me, let alone give me any suggestions to make my condition better.

I convinced my mother to take me to the chiropractor (which took a lot of pestering and begging because she was reluctant to do anything out of the typical child rearing duties).

Begrudgingly, she shuttled me to his office. This doctor thoroughly examined me. He listened to me when I explained that I had recently grown six inches in a year and a half, gaining no weight during this time, producing a lanky beanpole.

The doctor showed me how my hips rotated many degrees. He informed me that my weekly running of long distance miles during XC, compounded with hard long distance workouts and heavy sprint repeats for track, were pounding on my misaligned joints. This was causing inflammation and pain over and over again. My condition was becoming chronic and that was why it was not going away.

After a few intensive months of chiropractic treatment, he managed to get me out of pain. Amazing! I was now back to what I loved to do, which was running. It was truly a miracle. I am still an avid runner today. On a weekly basis, I run three to five days per week. This mostly depends on if I have any upcoming scheduled races. Accordingly, I seem to be always training. I usually do one long run per week, around six miles, just to keep my distance maintained so that when I do have a race it is an easier jumping off point.

I was a very competitive runner growing up, but after high school I did not run in college. Even though I was not on any organized team, I remained competitive with myself. I have gone through periods where I have diligently trained hard. In my late thirties, I was running in a lot of half marathons. I completed a full marathon when I was younger, but I did not like the time, energy, and commitment it took to train properly. Half marathons were easier for me to train and I excelled at that distance.

So I decided I wanted to really run a fast half marathon and I knew I would need direction. I hired a virtual coach, a gentleman named Matt who had a virtual and actual running business. One of my best friends went to college with him and they ran XC and track together. Matt was a collegiate All American.

Matt uploaded brutal workouts to a virtual calendar.

These included shorter and longer mile runs, quarter/half and mile/mile repeats on the track for time, hills and sprints, as well as intermittent runs with race pace miles dispersed among the distance. The half marathon race that I was training so hard to make my personal record, PR, was the Long Beach Half Marathon. It was a race I had done for many years with my cousin John and knew the course well. It had flat areas, some hills, and a nasty hill at mile nine that made you think a sadistic person designed the route.

I finished that race in 1:49, exactly the time I was shooting for. Even though I was so proud of myself that I trained that hard to accomplish this amazing time for me, it was such tough training that led up to an even more excruciating race. To get that 1:49 time, I fought for every second. I crossed the finish line and almost cried because I was in shock how exactly I hit my goal and the workouts it took to get there.

My now ex-husband raced that day too, and when he heard that I hit my time, he immediately said, "now you can hit 1:45 on your next race". That day I realized something. Although I had no regrets on how much effort I put forth to run my PR, all that work and obsession was turning running into more of a job and less of my decades long passion. From that day, I decided to not train so hard and get back to my love for running without some giant end goal.

Now I run for me, my pace, my time, and my

schedule. I also love to train to help others who maybe never ran, hate running or want to go for a longer distance or race. Having several friends that I have done this with, most of them still run today.

One of my best friends, Angie, was originally one of my employees at my clinic. We hired her at twenty-one years old. Angie loved soccer and hated running. We ended up playing soccer in the same women's league in our town. She could not understand why I was still running hard in the second half while Angie, fourteen years younger, was gasping for breath. I told her my secret was long distance running on a regular basis.

Months after that, she came to me at work and asked if I would help her start running long distances.

Angie warned me we would have to walk in the beginning. I did not care, I was just so happy she wanted to run! The brief walking during our runs was very finite. She quickly became a fast, talented distance runner. We have raced 5K, 10K, half and full marathons together. It has been a blast. Our last half marathon, Angie was three months pregnant, so we really had her daughter running with us too.

I have a dear friend, Toni, who happens to be blind from birth. We are only a year apart. She is a massage therapist and at the time, she was doing massage at my clinic. One day she approached me and said she was starting to run, losing weight, and enjoying it. Toni wanted to know if I would be her running partner.

We started running together, two miles at first, then more. It turned out we were the perfect match. I am her guide and innately tell her instructions, grab her arm when I think it is safer to hold onto me, and she instinctively trusts me and my direction. I had never run with a blind person before. We were in-sync; chatting and laughing the whole way. We have run everything from 5Ks to a half marathon together. I even had race t-shirts made for us, where the back of hers says, "Blind Runner Not Drunk", and mine reads, "Guide Dog". They always get attention and produce some good chuckles from other runners.

There is also Amber, who has been my loyal and amazing office manager for over a decade, and a dear friend. She really wanted to be in better shape, and did not do a lot of sports, so she asked if I would run and train her for a 5K. Years later, Amber and I have run several 5Ks with more in store!

Running has become an integral part of my life. It fascinates me to think the idea of running came from my desire to be in better conditioning for basketball. I altered my course ever so slightly and received a gift that will stay with me throughout my lifetime. During that shift in my life, I also discovered my profession and another passion, chiropractic. I wanted to be some type of doctor; an MD or veterinarian, both of them were in my sights. My life path deviation then injured me, and also allowed me to recover and go on to be a doctor and continue running, pain free.

5 DIVORCE

I was 33 and working for a doctor in San Francisco, who was an icon in our chiropractic profession. Doing things the opposite way, I tried to build my practice on my own for six years but was struggling, so I went to work for someone else. Dr. Davis saw me speak at a conference and this led to him paying me to speak to his patients at his clinic. I did not realize this doubled as a job interview. Soon after I moved up to San Francisco from North County San Diego and started working for him.

If I was not successful in this venture I decided I was going to quit chiropractic for good. The great news was not only was I successful at my position, but it gave me the tools and experience to start and run my own clinic in Simi Valley years later.

I was happy that everything was finally clicking for me as a chiropractor, but I realized I did not want to work that hard for someone else indefinitely. Through meditation and prayer, I also came to grips that I did not want kids and "the white picket fence" life. I decided I wanted to have some adventure and earn a living.

The plan was to place ads in high end yachting

magazines for a live aboard chiropractor. I could be their personal doctor, yet travel the world and get paid for it! My friend was coming into town and we were going snowboarding for the weekend in Lake Tahoe, so I decided to place the ad when I got back.

As life would have it, I met a man in one of the casinos in South Lake Tahoe. He lived in Texas but he was there on a gambling trip (and very charming, let's call him Eric). Eric had me gamble with his money. After I lost quite a bit in a short amount of time, I stopped. We enjoyed a few drinks and talked, but after a while my friend and I left for our hotel room. I had no idea that this man would be the one I would marry and go on such an adventure that would eventually end in chaos and turmoil.

I did not get married to get divorced. However, from our short six month courtship living in different states, me moving from San Francisco to Texas to be with him, there were already signs of trouble.

Eric brewed resentment towards me. He was controlling and stubborn to a bitter flaw. Eric's way was the *only* way, rarely entertaining other thoughts or ideas. From moving to Texas and being engaged for almost a year, to planning a destination wedding in Lake Tahoe, NV, there were fights, silent treatment (mostly from me because of my frustration), and lots of alcohol consumption. It was a relationship that became dark and headed for disaster even before we were married.

At our wedding I was so mad at him that I refused to say vows, I barely got out an "I do". Instead, I watched people play golf at a celebrity tournament across from where our ceremony was taking place. On the night of our wedding, we ended up in a fight in the elevator, with us sleeping as far away as we could in the hotel bed. Eric left early the next day without a note. I remembered him saying he wanted to go white water rafting with his family but he gave me no concrete confirmation of his plans. So I spent the day after my wedding with friends that were still in town while my new husband was gone all day and night with no communication.

The next day as we were embarking to Reno Airport for our honeymoon, he decided at the last minute we should repack our luggage. This snafu resulted in leaving terribly late for the airport (something he did all the time, purposefully, and relished in it). We ended up missing our flight, which was first class so we had to give that up on the first leg, and put on standby for a flight leaving five hours later. After a stop over in Dallas where he left the airport to meet with his nephew to *allegedly* get info on the honeymoon details, Eric barely made our connecting flight. Eventually, we arrived in Cabo San Lucas.

It was supposed to be one of the most special times in our new life together. It turned into three plus hours of driving in a taxi to three different resorts, searching for where our reservations actually were because he could not find our confirmation information. We finally ended up in the resort that I said was our honeymoon location the whole time (go figure). We spent four days of our week-long honeymoon sleeping in separate beds and spending the day drinking to forget our misery.

After returning from our honeymoon, our relationship continued to deteriorate. Eric's bouts of anger intensified; berating and belittling me at every chance he got. I have always been strong, so although I knew his tirades were untrue, the fact he would constantly hurl insults and jabs at me to dehumanize me was beyond hurtful. Sadly, I would spew anger and insults right back.

Shortly after our wedding, I moved back from Texas to California to join a partner and put together a multidisciplinary clinic. Eric did not move to California to be with me for over a year and a half. He bullied me into agreeing to buy a house in California that was way over our budget and took most of our income to pay the mortgage, taxes and utilities.

Three months after we bought this monstrosity, the California real estate market crashed and we would not have the opportunity to refinance to bring down our payment. At one point, our two mortgages were over $8000 per month. Eric would tell me something must be wrong with me, that I must not be that good of a

doctor because he had clients that were chiropractors

that made $300K plus, which was much more than I

was earning.

Eric was not one for my solutions either. Every time I

suggested we should short sell the house and rent until

we built our credit back up and housing prices came

down, he would say, "No, YOU wanted to come back

to California, you just need to make more money".

Mind you, our combined income was over $400K and

most of it was getting flushed down the drain with

mortgage/taxes/utilities and insurance. I loathed him.

Both my home life and my work life were terrible

partnerships. I was a broken person. The only constant

emotions were despair and hopelessness. I felt like the biggest loser on the planet because I was the one who created all of this chaos. All my hard work to get to a great place in life had led me to a black hole, where all my positivity and accomplishments were being sucked into a terribly sad abyss.

I tried to make it better; reminiscing about the amorous feelings I once had for Eric. Or thought I had. I begged to go to counseling, and after some time he begrudgingly obliged. After three fruitless sessions of him arguing with the counselor about how everything was my fault, we stopped attending. Eric claimed, "it was such bullshit anyway". My surge of digging into my positive outlook, trying to salvage our marriage

DR. CATHY HUNTER, D.C.

was met with a complete brick wall.

Things were progressively getting more intense. The anger increased and so did the violent behavior. There were scarily abusive events that bordered on pure insanity. These ranged from him "accidentally" shutting the garage door while knowing I was on a ladder beneath it so it would hit me square in the back, to hurling his wedding ring at my face and skimming my nose. Allowing myself to stoop to his level, one time on vacation I slapped him across the face because he could not apologize for leading us to snorkel in waters without lifeguards. As we snorkeled, I was adamant about staying in rescue distance. Low and behold, I almost drowned and he never tried to come back in the water to help me. What is horrible is there were so many more of those sick interactions. I knew it was a matter of time before it may be too late to leave.

I knew that I had to make changes in my life, and divorcing Eric took priority. Passivity would not work in my favor either; I had to leave him because he would never leave me, no matter how miserable he or I was. I contemplated separation for so long, knowing he would put up such an emotional and financial fight if I left. It was easier for me to kick the problem to the future and go on autopilot. But the abusive interactions kept coming. If I didn't leave soon I would have no chance at a healthy life again.

A conversation I had with my best friend hit me the

right way. It allowed me to shift my course, giving me the motivation to finally leave Eric. During my usual bitch session about my husband, my friend calmly said, "You know I'll be here for you whether you stay or go, but you are 44 years old. You can keep going like this for God knows how long. Before you know it, you'll be 54 years old and think of how much harder it will be to start again. You are still young and have your life ahead of you to make it how you really want it".

Although she had spoken similar words of wisdom toward me, the way she put it, finally resonated. That conversation sent me on a trajectory that gave me the necessary gumption to leave Eric for good.

Even though I wanted my divorce and it was the

right thing to do, it was still one of the hardest things I have ever done in my life. It was an incredible feeling of loss and the realization that I chose a life of disaster. Despite building my practice up and doing well financially, it was still terribly scary to let my financial and life partner go and be alone again.

There were so many unwarranted doubts and fears about what was to come. I wasn't even sure I could make it on my own again. I have never experienced such self-guilt and loathing. It was the knowledge that I married him, aware that there were problems, that caused me to beat myself up daily. Every aspect of our relationship was crap, and I did it all to myself. This is one of the reasons why it took me this long to build up the courage and end the marriage.

True to form, Eric dragged out our divorce for five years. This included five different court dates. During one session, I had to take him to court to have Eric sign a bifurcation requesting the court to deem me single and not married while we continued to hash out the financial details. On another occasion, I was questioned for just shy of two days during our divorce trial about why I took the Le Creuset cookware. Eric requested I reimburse him for half of the set, despite them being gifts from him.

It was a complete waste of time, money, and emotional peace. The divorce trial was the closest I have ever felt to being in prison and suppressed by someone else. I had to pay him for half of the value of my practice, even though I had permanently closed the business a few years prior.

I realized that divorce, at least in California, with no children involved, was basically a math problem. On paper it was simple: 50-50 split of assets and debts, and in this case no alimony because we made about the same income. However, his attorney was so nasty, she would throw any accusation or declaration of what he was owed, even if it had no legal backing.

Looking back now, it could have been easily done within a year. Add everything up and divide it by fifty percent. Instead, his beast of an attorney consistently took the offensive and led the case on its long, drawn out course. This cost us both tens of thousands of dollars and plenty of tears and misery on my behalf.

All those small shifts finally got me to leave him and our marriage. I left on a workday and had amazing friends and patients help me frantically pack up my belongings before the neighbors called him at work to tip him off that I was leaving. Eric knew I was going, but he did not know when. I was living in the spare bedroom for a few months and slowly packing boxes to get ready for the fateful day.

As I prepared to leave, I showed up everyday at my practice, running the place and seeing patients. I put feelers out to where I would move next. Because I was so scrambled mentally, I had no idea what I could afford. Needless to say, I wanted to keep it as cheap as possible. At first, I rented a room from a woman for a few months, and although the condominium was gorgeous, she was a nightmare so the search continued.

I asked some patients during this time if they knew of anyone who had a small guest house, or cottage for rent. My godsend place to live came from an unlikely patient. This patient had grown up in town and I figured he might know someone. Turns out, his family had a small rental house on hundreds of acres of a cattle and horse ranch that was about to be vacant.

My fear of leaving my husband led me to the most unexpected, perfect place to live. It was a small three bedroom home tucked away in a slot canyon. There were horses, cattle, peacocks, no cell phone service, and a solitude that I desperately needed to heal. It even had its own graveyard! I love a good spooky feature.

All of this, and only 3.5 miles from my practice at the time. I spent five years hidden in an area that could be mistaken for Montana in Southern CA. It was some of the best years of my life; adventure on a digestible scale. Like running away but never going too far.

I lovingly called my home, "Hunters Ranch". It gave me a quiet, safe place where I could be alone and reconnect with myself and nature. I had so much fun sharing my place with my friends, and even adopted my dog Rosie while living here. It was in those days where I soaked in my loneliness and breathed out my hurt as I prepared for the next step of my shifted life.

Hunters Ranch is where I finally came to grips with the realization that I was terrified to be alone. Not alone as in living alone, or loving time by myself, alone in the sense that I was all I had. No real partner, and definitely not settling for a mate that would betray me. I could not do that again. It was difficult to admit this to myself. It's bleak convincing yourself that you may never find that perfect person. My unfolding reality was accepting this fact, grieving it, wishing for different circumstances, and then swallowing it. By finally being okay with the notion that I may never have a perfect partner; with the very thing that scared the hell out of me, brought a sense of peace. It plugged up my internal wound that was not so visible to others who thought of how strong and independent I portrayed myself. Hunters Ranch was the place that allowed me to get to this next step and be ready for the future, even if it was solo.

Looking back at my marriage and divorce, all the drama it embodied, I never would have never imagined it leading me to a peaceful place. It delivered me to a hideaway that provided me the shelter to nurture and lick my wounds, growing new, more intelligent armor. I took it one day at a time, each day creating more roots to ground me in what was my authentic self again.

6 AF (ALCOHOL FREE)

It was May 2020, the Tuesday after Memorial Day. I was up early as usual, walking Rosie, when I got a phone call from my friend Peppa. I always get a little worried when people call at odd times, versus text. Peppa called to say hi and the conversation started as the usual gab about what we did over the weekend, and in particular for Memorial Day. We both relished in how wonderful the weather was, and we both did our share of hanging with friends and social drinking. Then the call took a turn.

The chat shifted to a dark place. Peppa lamented

how the whole covid situation: the stress, alienation, and fear, was turning into a breeding ground of increased bad behaviors. These included drinking more, unhealthy eating and decreased exercise. She was sick and tired of it and wanted to take matters into her own hands.

Peppa told me about a website she came across called OYNB, One Year No Beer. It was a company out of England that basically helped people become alcohol free through challenges of abstaining. Their tag line was, "Change Your Relationship With Alcohol And Watch Your Whole World Change". They had several challenges ranging from five days to 30/60/90 and even one year where you would not consume alcohol.

Peppa expressed interest in joining, and it was not that expensive.

For your price of admission, you received daily emails to feed you with information and help guide you on your journey. I could hear the excitement in her voice as she explained the challenges. Peppa wanted to do the 90 day one.

Peppa was not an alcoholic, far from it. She was like so many people, including myself, that wanted to make a positive change and do something that was outside the norm. Especially during covid, where the whole world was on its head, with fear, confusion and uncertainty spinning around everywhere.

Alcohol was at the forefront of covid. I witnessed an

abundance of commercials about alcohol and the escape of drinking. Memes were running wild where it seemed like alcohol was not just accepted but required to get through this covid mess. Peppa wanted an accountability partner, and she had to run through her list of friends to figure out who was crazy enough to accept the challenge. That is when she called me.

Looking back now, it seems funny that I was very hesitant at first to jump on board. For one, we were in this chaos of covid and it was nice to have alcohol as a buffer and escape. This was also a big year for me, I was turning 50 in July and we had a lot of big trips planned. We planned a canoeing trip down the Colorado River on a 6 person, privately guided tour with my niece and friends. For my actual 50th birthday, we were heading to an all inclusive resort in Puerto Vallarta to celebrate with more friends. How could I not drink during these festive vacations?

I decided to do the OYNB free five day challenge so I could inspect what this was all about. Although I wanted to do the challenge to be in solidarity with my dear friend, it was hard to let go and commit to the 90 day challenge. As I became very honest with myself, I knew deep down that I needed a break too. It was hard to admit that to myself.

So for the first five days, I read the OYNB emails and watched their videos. They were concise, informative and the presenters had adorable accents. They spoke candidly that alcohol was just another nasty drug. A drug dressed up in beautiful bottles and happy people drinking. Alcohol had all the nasty addictive properties as other drugs, but more accepted in society and even celebrated. It is not like this was shocking or even new to me, but it was the way they communicated it. They even said, "it's not your fault, it's the alcohol".

Those first five days hit me so hard in the best way. It all made perfect sense. I immediately signed up for the 90 day challenge and texted Peppa that I was all in. What was strange was although I was all in, I was terrified to tell my husband and other friends about this challenge. I was scared of their judgment. Would they think I was an alcoholic, or that I had a problem?

Would they not understand that I was still me, just an alcohol free me? I could not believe the personal mindf*ck. Again, it is easy to look back now and see how ridiculous those initial fears were. However, while I was going through it, especially those early days of AF (alcohol free), it was a confusing and scary time, on top of an already bewildering covid world.

You have to understand that prior to this challenge, I was *the* wine lady. I loved great wine, had lots of experience drinking and visiting tons of wineries. My palate had gotten very educated. My friends and ex-husband even started our own winery, Hunters Leap. I was the woman who brought the wine to the party, and I could party with the best of them. Now I was the

AF lady and I have to say it really confused some of my closest friends.

Peppa and I would text each other daily about what day we were on and how we felt. We would share our fears and our wins. Both of us experienced push back from our friends which included them questioning what we were doing. We realized our decision to be AF was making them uncomfortable, even though that was not our intention at all. Finally, we figured out that people were scared that we were not going to be as fun, as silly, or maybe even a stick in the mud. They acted so uncomfortable that the only conclusion we could come up with is that maybe they thought we were now going to start judging them for drinking.

That was never the case.

I remember telling my husband, Larry (my live-in boyfriend at the time) on AF Day 3. He had just mowed the lawn, and it was hot outside and he was sitting back, drinking an ice cold beer. I was so nervous to tell him of my decision. Even though I was strong in my commitment to see this AF challenge through the 90 days, as he sipped his beer I felt like a child who was told they could not have something. It was a dreadful fear of being left out. Weird. Like I said before, I did not even drink daily. Apparently, this is how much alcohol had an underlying grip on my life.

Not only was Larry beyond supportive, he was a little irked why I waited three days to tell him! This man supported anything I was into. I told him my fears and he said, "I think what you are doing is amazing"!

Everyday of being AF got easier. I was so thankful that I was not an alcoholic, only dealing with the social and mental issues of alcohol. I dove right into all the information. The OYNB daily emails and videos were great and I learned a ton from them. I read some AF books and they spoke directly to me. I resonated with the information about what alcohol does to your brain and body, as well as the social challenges of being AF. The OYNB podcast was fantastic too because they had experts, along with people just like me, talking about their journey, both pre and post AF.

As I tend to do when I go all in, I plunged into the AF

world. The OYNB Facebook group was amazing. Although I was reluctant at first (I am not a "group" type of person), I found it supportive and comforting. There were thousands of participants, all over the world.

I also joined the Facebook groups NABAS (Non-Alcoholic Beer Appreciation Society) and Non-Toxicated. This opened a whole new door of so many AF craft beers, AF spirits, AF wines, and drinks that it blew my mind. I went on the hunt for them and had so much fun finding them in local stores or buying them online. My refrigerator is now a bevy of AF choices, much like it had been before in the alcohol realm.

My friends still questioned why the hell I was doing

this. I am happy to report the general consensus was one of support and excitement for me. They finally put their fears away that I was judging them. It actually became the opposite, now I was the designated driver!

During the first 90 days, Larry would lovingly ask if it bothered me if he had a drink. I was so happy that it did not, but it was wonderful that he was so protective of my feelings. After a week or so, much earlier than I could have ever dreamed of, I started to look at alcohol the way I look at meat. I have been a "vegequarian" since my mid 20s (I give credit to my childhood friend, K for clarifying my state of eating: I do not eat meat, but eat fish/seafood/some dairy). My husband was having a margarita, I ordered an O'Douls, and as I watched him sip the drink, all I could think was how unappealing it was. That is how I think/feel when someone is eating a hamburger next to me. It does not bother me one bit, it may even smell delicious in some past reminiscent sense, but I have no desire to have one.

After the first few weeks, I felt so amazing mentally and physically that I considered never going back to drinking. It was a strange and uncomfortable thought at first. Alcohol had been a normal part of life. Not that I drank alcohol everyday, but more that alcohol had weaved its way through "ordinary" life. It ranged from witnessing my parents and relatives drinking on a regular basis, teen years of rebel drinking, college party days, to adult refined imbibing, which included my then obsession with wine (*hello* Hunters Leap).

Every occasion and non-occasion imaginable included alcohol. If you were sad, mad, happy, celebratory, or needed escape temporarily from just about anything, alcohol fit the bill. It was a learned behavior that I had adopted into my life. So the very thought of alcohol not being an option anymore was weird, but it also felt incredibly freeing. I could taste the liberation and I was not going back.

Being a doctor, and an aware adult, I was cognizant of the negative mental and physical health dangers of alcohol. Similar to so many others, I was fooling myself. I have always been physically active, and as an adult I still kept very active with my running and other sports like soccer, hiking, and hockey. All of these activities, along with my excellent eating habits and staying trim all these years were what I thought would protect me from any harm from drinking.

The few pounds I found lingering on my body for the past several years I chalked up to that perimenopause age, which is very unkind to women, especially in the weight gain arena.

I witnessed my mother drink herself to death. Towards the end of my mother's life, her liver had become so cirrhotic that a CT scan revealed the blood flow was going backwards because it could not get into the hardened organ. I was so mad at her about why she could not stop drinking knowing this deadly information. The liver has amazing regenerative properties, but my mother's did not because of the extensive damage.

My mom finally, reluctantly, and defiantly, did give up drinking about two years before she died. It was too little too late, the destruction was irreversible. My nieces and I would laugh that the only reason she lived for that long after her liver pretty much died was her diet of "donuts and denial". I gave up alcohol nine months after my mom died. I initially relinquished alcohol as a challenge because a friend really needed my help. Though the more I read and thought about it, my mother's death was the one of the final deciding factors on why I would not go back.

The ten pounds that flew off my body in the first 30 days of not drinking made me think what other terrible damage was going on inside of me. Realizing I never had to feel hungover, blackout, or regret the night before, were wonderful bonuses.

Now AF life is normal after three plus decades of alcohol intertwined into my life. At the time of this writing, I'm closing in on 1350 AF days. I've been more and more comfortable with being AF with every passing day. After about 60 days, I knew for sure this was my new normal. Around that milestone, Larry remarked, "You're not going to ever have a drink again, are you?". I smiled and shook my head no.

Over the next year I dealt with an interesting, awkward feeling. I didn't understand what it was. What I did know, was it had nothing to do with wanting or missing alcohol (thank god that was never an issue). I delved into this feeling, trying to define it and put my finger on what exactly made me so uncomfortable. This unsettling feeling was elusive because it took on different emotional depths. Sometimes it was boredom, other times it felt underwhelming. A few times it felt like I wanted to crawl out of my own skin. In the beginning when I recognized this nagging feeling, I tried to push it away because there is nothing more intense than dealing with strong emotions when you are stone cold sober. This perception persisted and allowed me time to sit with it so that I could define it.

This mystery emotion turned out to be the silence and stillness of my mind. My brain had an enormous amount of free space that was idle. Before this space was filled with the business of drinking and my mind swirling in that foggy space. What has been fun is harnessing this space to be more thoughtful, creative and overall, more productive. I do not have regrets about alcohol being in my life before this. I am living proof that the everyday persistence of leaving a behavior that did not serve me anymore built upon itself until it blossomed to my new way of life. I am so excited to live the rest of my life being unchained from alcohol and the culture that used to be my norm. Now that my mind is freed from those tethers, I am thrilled to see what I get into next.

7 THE FIVE DEGREES TO YOUR FUTURE OR

THE FIVE PILLARS

Well it's time to get started! First, you will need a foundation for The Five Degrees to your Future (or Five Pillars). You can use this as a plan to engineer your life the way you want it. These pillars are your own personal road map. They will give you the structure to follow your own path to make your life the way you want it.

You can use these simple effective steps to provide structure to keep you focused and ultimately, get you to the finish line. If it's easy, it's doable. I have learned that if it's complicated, you tend to let your goal fall by the wayside.

Pillar I – Decision

If you haven't already, it's time to ask yourself some questions. What do you want to do? Something big? Huge? Maybe just a small change in your life that you have been wanting to do but haven't followed through? It all starts with figuring out what you want. I'm giving you permission to dream big. You need to figure out what you want to accomplish so it has to start with something. Even a small change could be a big thing, it's all relative.

Think about the things you have already accomplished in your life. My decision to move to California started when I was 3 years old. It all emerged from a family road trip. Apparently my dad thought it was a great idea to pile all six of us (mom, dad, two grandmothers, myself and my brother) into our little station wagon and drive cross country from New Jersey to California. Road trips were common for families back then because few could afford to fly everyone 3000 miles.

We eventually arrived in Southern California, Cypress to be exact. The home of my Uncle Joe (dad's brother), Aunt Sue and my three cousins, Johnny, Mickey and Lori. I barely remember this trip but the memory of being blown away still is fresh in my mind. California was a foreign land, laden with palm trees, glitz, glimmer, and a lot of action. This was so much different than living in Sayreville, New Jersey, a small suburban east coast town with not much going on.

When I was nine, we embarked on another cross country trip. This time my dad was going to have us travel in style. One day my dad surprised all of us by pulling up in a Coachman motorhome. I remember my mom being so pissed off at him! Clearly, he surprised her too.

My mom was an elementary school teacher and had summers off, and my dad owned his own electrician business. This organically set the stage for a long cross country trip of a lifetime. This six week road trip rounded out the continental United States. We headed from New Jersey, down to Florida, then across the southern states, to once again Southern California, visiting my family. I was older, and much more impressionable.

I thought my California family was the coolest. How could they not be?! They lived down the street from Knott's Berry Farm and Disneyland. It was a short, fifteen minute drive to the beach too. I was mesmerized by the swaying palm trees and near perfect weather. I clearly remember declaring to my mom, "I'm going to live here when I get older".

That impactful decision stayed with me throughout

my growing up until I actually made it happen when I was twenty three years old. I finished my undergraduate education at Rutgers College, then knocked off additional prerequisite classes at Middlesex Community College. At the end of the summer of 1993, I went to Southern California to start chiropractic school at the Los Angeles College of Chiropractic in Whittier. That little decision I made as a kid shaped how I lived my life and the path I was taking to eventually relocating to CA when I was an adult. I never looked back.

I give you permission to do what YOU want. Go crazy. Get a piece of paper. Sit by yourself. Ask the simple but BIG question, "What do I want?". It's what

YOU want, not what your spouse, kids, friends or anyone other than you want. Be selfish. Sit down for 15 minutes, put a timer on, and write out what you want. You can spitball and write a ton of stuff down, just let the ideas flow. It does not matter how significant, trivial or how many ideas you get onto the paper. What matters is that you are putting stuff from your head into reality and into your focus. Now, you have a smorgasbord of ideas, goals, habits that you can decide to bring into your life.

Pillar II – Dedication (and Focus)

Alright, you have made your decision. Now, you

need to have the dedication to follow through and actually attain your goal. As they say, Rome was not built in a day. It takes serious dedication and focus to stay on course. As we all know, you can be laser focused and committed but for whatever reason you get thrown off your way. However, if you have a plan for when you get off course you can pick yourself back up and get focused again.

The key is to accept that life happens and you will lose your way. Success is having a plan to get back on track when the blip arises. Your plan is like leaving a light on that can help bring you back when you wandered too far off. Although my path took twists and turns and even led me to possibly not moving to

California, the core decision to move there was ingrained in my psyche for years. That influenced my decisions that finally got me to my destination, California. My dedication got me to finally pull the trigger and leave home. If I did not have that deep commitment, I would have never made it to California.

Think about your decision and realize the type of dedication that will keep you on that path. When things get tough, and you feel shaky about your goal, remind yourself of why you are taking on this goal in the first place. Your dedication will keep you going strong and your focus will help you from veering off your path, and bring you back when you inevitably sway.

Pillar III – Consistency

Consistency is the secret sauce to get you to success: doing the same things over and over. When you are consistent, it allows you to gather momentum. If you do not have the wheels turning, it is difficult to go forward. When you are trying to accomplish any goal, you definitely need momentum to carry you through.

We all hear a lot about willpower. It is powerful, but it will only get you through the short term. If all you have is willpower, you will burn out. You need more ammunition for the long haul. This is where consistency and momentum will continue you on the path to your goal. Consistency is also a building block. When it is compounded, consistency creates cumulative effects. Consistency + momentum = cumulative effects.

When I started my undergraduate education at Rutgers College, I knew my next stop would be chiropractic college and California. I did not know my path would shift when I met my first real boyfriend, Alex. Alex was my first love and we fell hard for each other.

Alex was studying to become an engineer and moving to California was not on his path. My nineteen year old self could not imagine life without him. So, I decided to change my major to Economics because my

DR. CATHY HUNTER, D.C.

roommates were all in those classes and they seemed to like them. I even looked into going to chiropractic school in New York, closer to our New Jersey home.

Our relationship finally fizzled my junior year, and my dislike for economics grew. I watched my roommates wearing sharp business suits and going for internship interviews. I imagined doing the same, and finally landing a job in a cubicle in some tall building. That goal did not excite me, and I realized there was no way that was for me. So I went back to my original plan of school in California.

While my friends were taking it easy our senior year with filler classes, I was taking difficult science prerequisites. I knew I would have enough credits to graduate in my planned four years of college. However, my divergence off my California path would cost me another year of prerequisite classes at our local community college. So as I took those three classes I had left to finish, I worked my tail off being a server and saving my money for California. Thank goodness I had my original plan to fall back on!

As you go on your journey and stay consistent with whatever you are attempting to accomplish, you begin to witness more positive changes related to your goal. This leads to noticeable results. Witnessing changes that you made on your path will keep you motivated to continue. You will be amazed how into your goal you will become. Seeing results just fuels your fire to keep going and get more of the same. It's the good type of being obsessed with something.

What will it take for you to be consistent so that you can gather momentum enough to see the results you want to achieve? That is very unique for you and your goals, and only you can define this. It has to embody observable changes that occur when you are putting in the work day after day.

Pillar IV – Celebration

Celebration does not have to be a giant party. It's more of the everyday little celebrations that are so important to keep you going. It is like putting little nuggets of fun along the way. By giving yourself rewards, or something to look forward to, you can make it into an entertaining little game.

Put a trip on the calendar, a lunch date, or perhaps that perfect present to yourself. Then you know how many days away this treat is, and you have to work that much more to get to your reward. I believe this is a huge part of what a lot of people miss on their road to their goals. It's the little everyday celebrations that are motivating and fun. Going toward your goal does not have to be serious and so Type A that it becomes a chore. You should have fun along the way.

What happened to fun? If you watch kids, they play, they get into everything and their little minds expand. They are free beings. Then you get older, you get a job, you get bills, maybe have kids, and the adulting list goes on and on. Life can get bogged down with stress and become mundane. With all of that responsibility, the thought of even starting something new can be too much to handle, especially when you are setting somewhat lofty goals for yourself.

Even a small change can seem insurmountable when you have regular life to deal with on top of it. You can experience setbacks and it can be overwhelming. If you do not have those milestones to celebrate, well frankly, then it's just not that fun. Where we are headed with our pillars and the five degrees to your future is about freedom. Freedom is packed with fun because it means you get to choose what you want for your life. That sounds like a fun time to me!

Don't you want to live a life of significance? The meaning of that is extremely personal to each one of us. You don't have to be president, or CEO, but what significance means to you. Much like results, relishing in those victories, big or small, will continue your motivation to keep you on the path to the finish line. Lighten up and enjoy the ride.

Pillar V- Vision/Opportunities

It's amazing the people you meet, the experiences you have, the other ideas that pop into your head all because you started on one tangent. Be successful, take care of yourself and others and have a fun time while doing it. As long as you continue on the path to your goal, it will be an entertaining ride.

So now you have read real life examples from my own life adventures. The hardest part about starting anything is just that – starting. That is no joke. The paralysis that occurs when you become overwhelmed by the enormity of starting something new can be terrifying. It will stop you dead in your tracks. That is why it is so imperative that you simply begin. The easiest way to get moving is by dipping your toe in and starting small. Point your ship in the direction you want to go and just push off the dock. You will be amazed how far you travel from the mainland.

One of the magical bonuses I have witnessed going through this transformational process is how open your brain becomes. Once you start off on that new task, or are training yourself in a new habit, your brain starts recognizing other changes that are even possible. These possibilities may not have even been in your awareness before you began. It is like your neurons start firing all over the place, and now all your brain can do is come up with all the additional ways you can compliment and even expand this new goal.

In general, I am a positive, glass-is-full kind of gal, but for about six months or so, this weird indifference was running a thread through my life. I had a hard time defining it, but I realized it was apathy. It was clouding even my banner days, this dullness was bringing down my joy. The worst part was although I identified it, I couldn't shake that indifferent feeling away.

I felt tremendous guilt when my mother died. While she was dying, laying listless in her hospital bed, with only her breath heaving her body, it was so brutal. My nieces, who were there with us, were super close to their grandmother. They were looking to me as the elder/leader on how to deal with this, and all I could do was offer support over my own terror.

We left the hospital one night, and really thought she would not make it to the next morning. However, when we returned around noon the next day she was still in the dying mode. I felt so guilty I left her alone all night. I really struggled with this for about a year, but mostly when I had a few drinks is when the overwhelming feelings hit me. I would beat myself up with that guilt and cry my eyes out. All of that emotion seemed to be in vain because the guilt would never be washed away.

When I became AF (alcohol free), having zero alcohol made me observe and deal with feelings better. I knew logically I was just doing the best thing at the time, and she knew we were there and we loved her. So after 90 days or so being AF, when I pondered this whole guilt thing, I was able to let it go and not revisit it because of no alcohol clouding my brain and feelings!!!

I call it my journey from Apathy to Happify: my brush with this terrible feeling and my adventure back to pollyanna-ville. If I never accepted the no alcohol challenge from my friend, and then embraced it as a lifestyle, I would probably still be playing those guilt tapes over and over in my head. The AF path led me to the let go of the guilt path that I am so grateful for today.

I cannot tell you the number of times I was focused toward one goal, and along the way so many other great ideas as well as additions to whatever I was working on. You have to remember to stay open to things around you, even when you are laser focused on something else. I truly believe we as humans were born for this: live our best lives the way we truly want to.

8 WHAT'S NEXT AND DEALING

WITH CHANGE

We have been on a journey to reveal to you that anything is possible. You have to adhere to that unlimiting belief because the negative will try to ease its way into your plans at some point. So your positive attitude is a must to begin.

Pick something you've been wanting to do, or perhaps previously started but gave up. If passion is gnawing at you still, you need to pursue it. If you keep talking about something, then you really need to do it. Talk is a nice starting point but you must apply action or the words will ultimately bore and frustrate you if they are not put into motion. A great start is to join groups for motivation and inspiration. Facebook is a great resource. Personally, I was not into this at first. However, when I started my AF journey, I joined the OYNB (One Year No Beer) Facebook group, as well as NABAS (Non-Alcoholic Beer Appreciation Society) and Non-Toxicated groups. The support, ideas, and sense of community were positively overwhelming. It was extremely encouraging how many people were going through the same adventure as myself, with all its challenges, exhilarations and setbacks.

These groups were also amazing for accountability. Having a buddy or partner that can help you stay on track is just one more tool to keep you moving forward. This accountability person can be a friend working toward the same goal. Facebook groups give you access to thousands of people on the same path. Ultimately, it is your own journey. It's a solo mission that only you can follow through. However, inviting people on your journey in snippets helps keep you accountable and committed. You have to do what is necessary to get you to the finish line.

I've shared from my own personal experiences that you can really shape your life the way you want it. Yes, there are challenges, obstacles and all sorts of twists and turns. But if you keep moving forward, little by little, and adjusting your course as needed, you will get there eventually. How fast your trajectory will run is really up to you, your choices, commitment and actions.

My Five Degrees to Your Future is your outline to apply to your own goals. This structure will destroy procrastination because it is your plan. The best part about the Pillars is you can customize them and apply them to anything you want to accomplish. Start small, go big, it is really up to you. It has always been up to you; either you did not realize that or maybe life has just beat you up enough to give up on your dreams and live an ordinary life. Well, not anymore!

One of my dearest friends, Maureen, was my buddy for fifteen years. We were twenty years apart, but had gotten so close, especially after we both got divorced. She had just turned 70 in February 2020. Just a few years before her big birthday milestone, she had gotten divorced after being married for over three decades. Although she was thriving in her newly single life, she was still working away, saving for retirement and looking to the future.

Her health was compromised for many years, but somehow she toiled on, down playing it as bad acid reflux and stomach issues. It ended up being stage IV gastric cancer. With that news, she even went through a massive cancer removal surgery. Maureen survived the surgery and three weeks in the hospital, determined as ever to make a full recovery and get on with her life. Her new phase of life would also include finally retiring.

Maureen was following a woman on TikTok who was about her age. This retired lady bought a motorhome and was venturing forth to gear up to travel the country. Maureen dreamed about doing that. She also wanted to move from Southern California to Blowing Rock, North Carolina, an idyllic mountain town near her daughter. We laughed at how I would go visit her there, or anywhere.

Unfortunately, within a few weeks after coming

home from the hospital, she passed away. Maureen died in her favorite chair in her beautiful apartment that she loved. She passed away in August 2020, and up to that point saved quite a nest egg. Although her passing was not a total shock, given her diagnosis and the surgery she endured, it was still quite a blow. Especially for me to be on the scene the day she died. I was with her daughter and friend as we said goodbye to her in the body bag. It was so surreal. Somehow it still seems like she just went away, rather than she actually died.

I'll never forget standing in her apartment courtyard, talking amongst her other friends about how sad this was. Her close friend, Mike, who was there, was also her financial planner. Mike shook his head. He could not believe that not only was she gone, but all that money she saved she would never get to enjoy. It was depressing on all counts.

Maureen was one of my besties gone too early. She had plans and had enough money to carry them out. Maybe if she would have more proactively handled those stomach symptoms that started years ago she would be here today: in her motorhome following us on all sorts of adventures. The point of sharing Maureen's story is to drive home the point of you have one life, so go live it. Make it yours. Don't be a victim. If you don't like something about yourself, or how your life is going, then take the necessary steps to change it.

Don't wait too long to live the life you truly want. That's why I wrote this book. Life can be a grand adventure. And it's even more sweet when you design it that way. Sure, there will be ups and downs on the roller coaster of life. If you have a plan in place, you will be able to navigate when you veer off your course.

Life does have one guarantee – it will end eventually. So how do you want to live it? My mom once said that life was just one big party for Cathy Hunter. I now take that as a compliment because I attempt to engineer it that way. Embrace the fear, change slowly, and toast to your success!

I want nothing but the best for you. Go after those dreams and enjoy the ride...

DR. CATHY HUNTER, D.C.

ABOUT THE AUTHOR

DR. CATHY HUNTER, D.C. HAS BEEN A PRACTICING CHIROPRACTOR SINCE 1997, AS WELL AS AN AUTHOR, LECTURER, INVENTOR AND PASSIONATE ABOUT LIVING LIFE TO THE FULLEST. SHE HAS BEEN A MENTOR TO HER PATIENTS, FRIENDS, FAMILY AND EVEN STRANGERS ON BEING POSITIVE AND OVERCOMING ANY CHALLENGES THAT LIFE BRINGS YOUR WAY. HER LIFELONG THIRST FOR LEARNING AND CREATING KEEPS HER BUSY.

DR. HUNTER IS MARRIED TO THE LOVE OF HER LIFE, LARRY GLOVER, IS A PROUD AUNT TO HER NIECES AND NEPHEWS, AS WELL AS A DOG MOM TO ROSIE. SHE LOVES THE OUTDOORS, IS AN AVID CAMPER/RV LIFESTYLE ENTHUSIAST, RUNNER, HIKER, PICKLEBALL PLAYER AND ANYTHING THAT GETS HER INTO NATURE.

SHE IS THE OWNER OF HUNTER HOLISTICS CBD COMPANY, AS WELL AS THE HOST OF "FIVE DEGREES TO YOUR FUTURE" PODCAST.

WWW.SHOPHUNTERHOLISTICS.COM

WWW.THEFIVEDEGREES.COM

www.ingramcontent.com/pod-product-compliance
Lightning Source LLC
Chambersburg PA
CBHW051730040426
42447CB00008B/1059